GEOGRAPHICS

ANIMALS

The Illustrated Geography of Our World

RESEARCHED AND WRITTEN BY
SUSAN MARTINEAU

DESIGNED AND ILLUSTRATED BY
VICKY BARKER

FOR YOUNG READERS

Racehorse for Young Readers

A BIOME TO CALL HOME

Planet Earth is home to millions of animals. The world has many types of land and climate, from freezing cold mountains to wet and hot forests. These different areas are called biomes. Let's have a look at some of them and the animals who live there.

DESERTS

Have less than **10 inches** rain **EACH YEAR.**

HOTTEST desert air temperature

134°F

was recorded in Death Valley, USA.

The Antarctic and Arctic are **COLD DESERTS.**

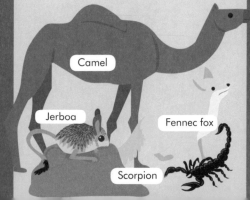

Camel

Jerboa

Fennec fox

Scorpion

POLAR ZONES

Arctic - - - - - - -

- - - - - Antarctica

It is **DARK** for **6 MONTHS** a year.

The air is so **COLD** your breath makes **ICE CRYSTALS.**

ANTARCTICA
There are no land animals here BUT lots in the ocean.

Weddell seal

Adélie penguin

Orca

ARCTIC

Polar bear

Walrus

Narwhal

Harp seal

WETLANDS

This is land that is **ALWAYS** covered by **WATER,**

like **BOGS, SWAMPS,** and **MARSHES.**

FRESH or **SALT**

BRACKISH
(a mixture of fresh and salt)

Wetlands are **ESSENTIAL** snack bars for thousands of migrating birds.

Flamingo

Heron

Fish

Alligator

WORKING WITH ANIMALS

A **HABITAT SPECIALIST** works in wildlife parks and zoos to make sure that animals have the surroundings and homes they need. They can help to set up safe places for endangered creatures, too.

Animals can be
VERTEBRATES or **INVERTEBRATES**

= | =
Animals with a backbone. | Animals without a backbone.

97% of animals are invertebrates.

TROPICAL RAINFORESTS

These are found between the Tropic of Cancer and the Tropic of Capricorn.

Tropic of Cancer

Equator

Tropic of Capricorn

HOT and **WET**

There is more rain here in **2 DAYS** than there is in a desert in **1 YEAR.**

More than **HALF** of **ALL** animal species live here.

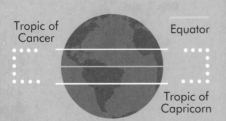

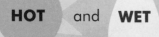

Three-toed sloth

Toucan

Tree frog

Army ant

GRASSLANDS

These have more rain than deserts, but not enough to grow many trees.

Grasslands have the **LARGEST** herds of animals, **BIGGEST** and **FASTEST** land animals, and **BIGGEST** birds on Earth.

Ostrich 9 feet

Tall man 6.5 feet

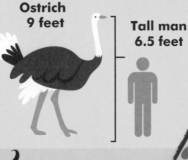

Springbok

Giraffe

Lion

Zebra

MOUNTAINS

It gets **COLDER** and **COLDER** as you go up a mountain.

EVERY 3,280 feet UP

= **50°F drop.**

There are also **STRONG** winds

and **LESS** oxygen to breathe.

O_2

Ibex

Golden eagle

Mountain lion

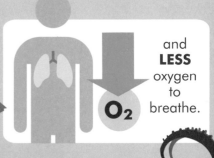

Alpine marmot

OCEAN DEPTHS

Many amazing animals live in our oceans and seas. So far, scientists have named about 250,000 (a quarter of a million) species, but they think there are so many more to discover! Who knows what else lives in the very deepest depths?

656 feet

EPIPELAGIC or SUNLIGHT ZONE

Sunlight still reaches down into the water here.

MESOPELAGIC or TWILIGHT ZONE

It is getting very dark as the water gets deeper.

3,280 feet

BATHYPELAGIC or MIDNIGHT ZONE

The only light here is from glowing **(BIOLUMINESCENT)** creatures.

13,123 feet

ABYSSOPELAGIC ZONE

Here it is **DARK** and **FREEZING COLD.**

❄ ❄ ❄ ❄

19,685 feet

HADOPELAGIC ZONE

Here are **DEEP VALLEYS** in the oceans called **TRENCHES.**

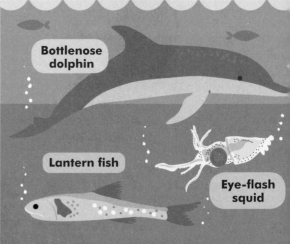

Bottlenose dolphin

Lantern fish

Eye-flash squid

Deep-sea spider crab

Vampire squid

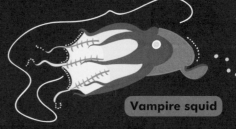

The **DEEPEST** trench found so far is the **Mariana Trench** = 36,201 feet.

WORKING WITH ANIMALS

MARINE BIOLOGISTS study all kinds of sea and ocean creatures from whales to microscopic plankton. They look at the way marine animals live together. They also investigate how pollution and climate change affect these creatures.

SURFACE
The flying fish glides through the air to escape predators!

 Jellyfish

Clownfish

Humpback whale

Tiger shark

Viperfish

Giant Pacific octopus

Sperm whales can dive to about **0.6 miles DEEP.** They can hold their breath for **90 minutes.**

Gulper eel

Fangtooth

Sea pig

The **DEEPER** you go the **MORE** the water presses down on you. **8,200 feet** deep = same as an elephant standing on your toe!

Angler fish

Snailfish

ANIMAL LIVES

Some animals live for much longer than others. Animals in zoos and pet animals usually live longer than the ones in the wild. All animals have babies. Some babies grow inside the mother animal's body before being born alive. Other animals lay eggs with babies inside them.

There are 5 groups of **VERTEBRATES** (animals with backbones):

Mammals

Have warm blood.

Need to breathe air.

Most live on land.

Some live in water (whales and dolphins).

Birds

Have wings with feathers. Most can fly.

Fish

Live in fresh or salt water.

Amphibians

Can live on land or in water.

Have cold blood.

Reptiles

Have cold blood.

Need the Sun to warm them.

	GESTATION or INCUBATION	NUMBER OF BABIES
LONG-TAILED SHREW	**21 days** (3 weeks)	**2-5 babies**
DOG	**2 months** (9 weeks)	**3-6 puppies** (but sometimes can be up to 10!)
HORSE	**11 months**	**1 foal**
POLAR BEAR	**8 months**	**2 cubs** (stay with mom for up to 3 years)
BOTTLENOSE DOLPHIN	**1 year**	**1 calf**
AFRICAN ELEPHANT	**22 months**	**1 calf**
GIANT TORTOISE	babies hatch out after **8 months**	lays **25 eggs**

WORKING WITH ANIMALS

VETERINARIANS and **VETERINARY NURSES** look after animals when they are sick or need an operation. They might work with pets like dogs, cats, and hamsters, or treat animals like rhinos and giraffes in wildlife reserves.

Elephant babies stay with their moms for **10 YEARS.** This is longer than any other animals apart from humans!

The Greenland shark is **OVOVIVIPAROUS** = eggs hatch INSIDE the mother shark and then the baby sharks are born.

AVERAGE LIFE SPAN

18 MONTHS

8-15 YEARS

10 pups

might live up to 400 YEARS!

25-30 YEARS

25-30 YEARS

up to 45 YEARS

70 YEARS

up to 200 YEARS!

EXTREME SURVIVAL

Some animals make their homes in habitats, or surroundings, where it is more difficult to survive.
Over time, they have to adapt, or change, to be able to live there.
Here are just a few extreme places and amazing animal adaptations.

Polar bear

The world's **LARGEST** bear = **8 feet** long.

THICK BLUBBER (fat) under fur to keep warm.

FUR UNDER PAWS to grip snow and ice.

Arctic fox

CAMOUFLAGED fur is **WHITE** in winter and **DARK** in summer.

FANTASTIC HEARING to listen for prey under the snow.

THICK, FURRY TAIL to use as a duvet.

Lemming

BURROWS under snow to keep warm and **HIDE** from predators.

Arctic

Antarctica has no native **LAND** animals.

POLAR

Southern elephant seal

Lots of **BLUBBER** to keep warm.

18 feet long and **WEIGHS** as much as **2 CARS.**

Penguin

BRILLIANT DIVER and **SWIMMER** in freezing ocean.

Snow leopard

THICK fur to keep warm.

GREY coat for **CAMOUFLAGE** against rocks and snow.

WORKING WITH ANIMALS

EVOLUTIONARY BIOLOGISTS are scientists who study the history of life on Earth. They look at how animals have changed over time to suit their environment. They also research how animals interact (live together).

WETLANDS

Okavango Delta, Botswana, Africa.

DESERT

Sonoran Desert, North America.

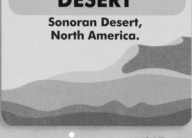

Gila woodpecker

Makes **NESTS** inside cactus plants.

Yellow-billed stork

LONG bill to catch fish.

LONG legs to wade through the water.

Ringtail cat

NOCTURNAL
=
it only comes out at night to hunt when it is cooler.

Sidewinder rattlesnake

MOVES SIDEWAYS so only a small amount of its body touches the hot sand at one time.

HORNS above eyes to keep sand out of them.

Lechwe antelope

VERY LONG back legs to run through water to escape from predators.

MOUNTAINS

Himalayas, Asia.

Here are the world's highest mountains, including Mount Everest.

Himalayan pika

Looks like a **FURRY EGG** and even has **FURRY FEET** to keep warm.

LIVES in crevices in rocks.

Crocodile

MAKES TUNNELS AND DENS under floating papyrus beds to hide from danger and store its prey.

Golden eagle

HUGE WINGSPAN
=
up to **7.5 feet** to make the most of warm air rising up mountains to fly really **HIGH**.

GREAT EYESIGHT to see prey miles away AND loves to eat...

AMAZING MIGRATIONS

Some animals go on very long journeys every year. These journeys are called migrations. Some animals migrate to search for food or warmer weather. Others travel vast distances to have their babies in the same place every year.

ARCTIC TERNS

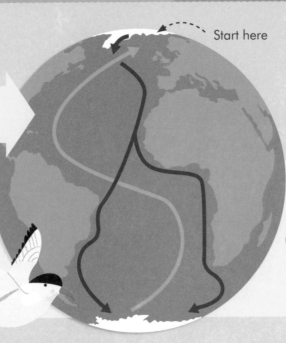

Start here

Migrate from the Arctic to the Antarctic and back again each year.

RETURN trip
=
48,000 miles

Terns can sleep while gliding.

During its lifetime the little tern flies

 **3 TIMES**

the distance from Earth to the Moon.

ADÉLIE PENGUINS

Go North for the winter and return South for the summer.

AVERAGE
return trip
=
8,100 miles

Antarctica

They have the longest migration of all penguins.

N
W · E
S

LONGEST
return trip
=
10,900 miles

ORNITHOLOGISTS study everything to do with birds. They sometimes work in very wild places to research bird migrations, nesting habits, and bird life cycles. You can be a bird scientist yourself with a pair of binoculars and lots of patience!

LONDON to NEW YORK
=
3,470 miles

WILDEBEEST

are also called gnus (ger-noos).

Their **CIRCULAR ROUTE** in East Africa is called **THE GREAT MIGRATION.**

TOTAL round trip
=
1,800 miles

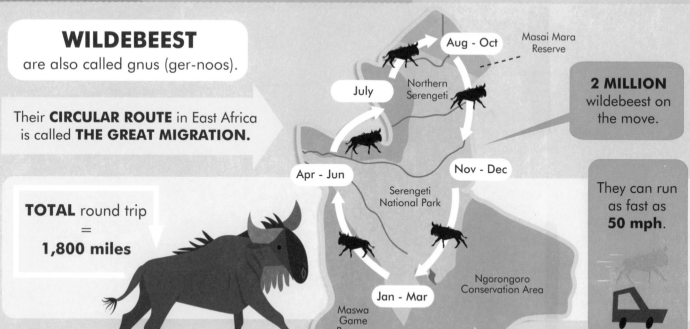

Aug - Oct

Masai Mara Reserve

July

Northern Serengeti

Apr - Jun

Nov - Dec

Serengeti National Park

Jan - Mar

Ngorongoro Conservation Area

Maswa Game Reserve

2 MILLION wildebeest on the move.

They can run as fast as **50 mph**.

GREY WHALES

Migrate from the Arctic to Mexico and back again.

RETURN trip for **ADULT WHALES**
=
10,000 miles

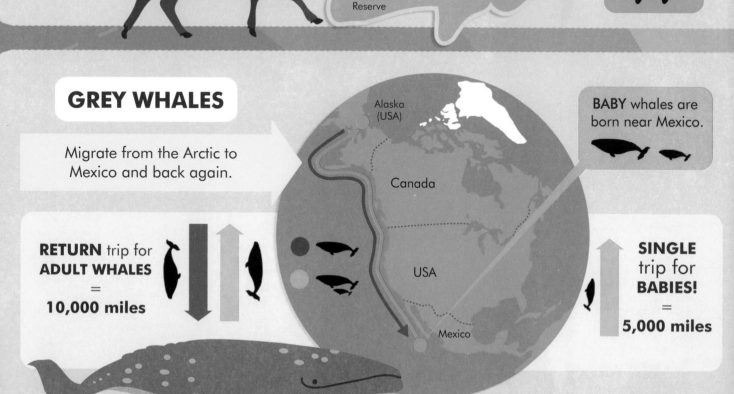

Alaska (USA)

Canada

USA

Mexico

BABY whales are born near Mexico.

SINGLE trip for **BABIES!**
=
5,000 miles

SUPERFAST ANIMALS

Animals adapt to where they live and sometimes this also means that they become really speedy to catch the prey they like to eat. Other animals have to be fast to avoid being eaten! There are some speed champions amongst them all.

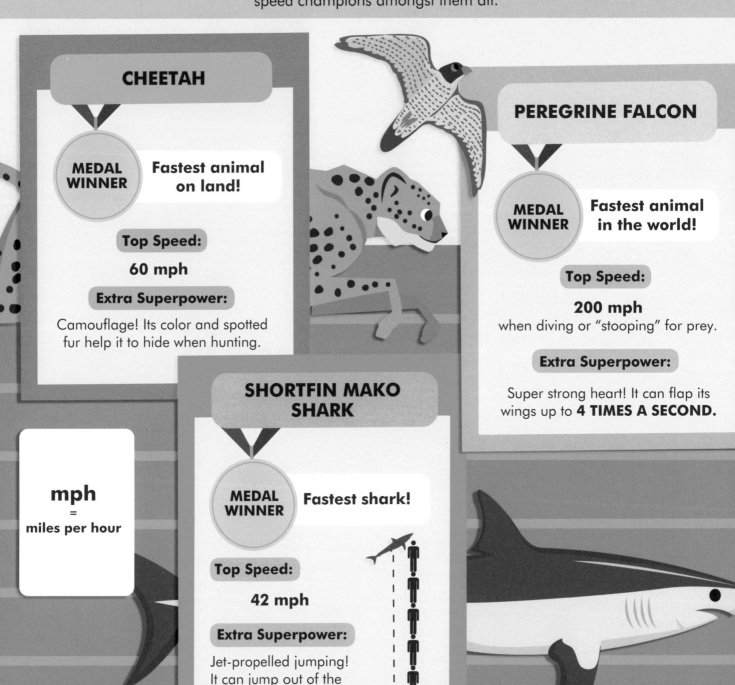

CHEETAH

MEDAL WINNER — **Fastest animal on land!**

Top Speed:

60 mph

Extra Superpower:

Camouflage! Its color and spotted fur help it to hide when hunting.

PEREGRINE FALCON

MEDAL WINNER — **Fastest animal in the world!**

Top Speed:

200 mph
when diving or "stooping" for prey.

Extra Superpower:

Super strong heart! It can flap its wings up to **4 TIMES A SECOND.**

SHORTFIN MAKO SHARK

MEDAL WINNER — **Fastest shark!**

Top Speed:

42 mph

Extra Superpower:

Jet-propelled jumping! It can jump out of the water up to **30 feet.**

mph
=
miles per hour

WORKING WITH ANIMALS

PARK NATURALISTS work in wildlife parks. Their job is to teach visitors about how all the animals behave and live together in a park. They get to spend lots of time outdoors!

Fastest HUMAN RUNNER

Usain Bolt

Top Speed: nearly 28 mph

SAILFISH

MEDAL WINNER — **Fastest fish!**

Top Speed:

Estimated to jet through water at same speed as a cheetah on land!

Extra Superpower:

Fantastic flexible fin! It can flatten the huge fin on its back to go faster.

DRAGONFLY

MEDAL WINNER — **Fastest insect in the world!**

Top Speed:

35 mph

Extra Superpower:

Zippy mover! It can fly up, down, backwards, and sideways to catch prey in mid-air.

OSTRICH

MEDAL WINNER — **Fastest bird that cannot fly!**

Top Speed:

45 mph

Extra Superpower:

Brilliant eyesight! Its eyes are **5 TIMES BIGGER** than a human's eye.

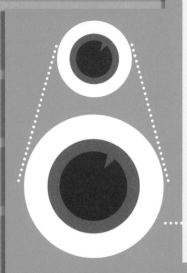

TREASURE ISLANDS

Some places on Planet Earth are home to very special animals. These creatures cannot be found anywhere else in the world. They are called "native," or "endemic," species. One of these amazing places is an island called Madagascar. But how did these animals get there in the first place?

160 MILLION years ago

There was a huge supercontinent called Gondwana. The land that became Madagascar was inside it.

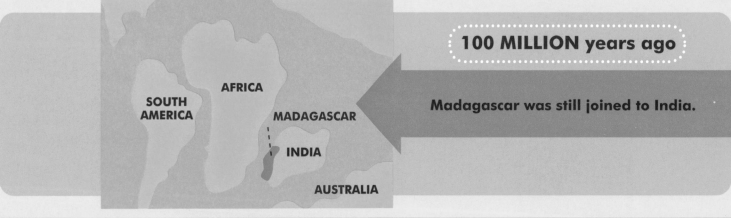

100 MILLION years ago

Madagascar was still joined to India.

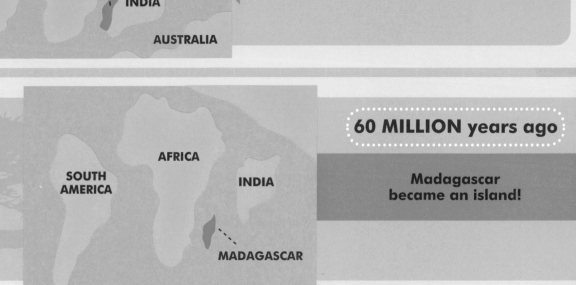

60 MILLION years ago

Madagascar became an island!

WORKING WITH ANIMALS

WILDLIFE FILM-MAKERS make films about animals. They can show us so much about animals we might never see in the wild ourselves. They can also show us how humans damage or hurt animals by destroying their homes or hunting them.

Giraffe weevil

Madagascar's animals
EITHER

stayed on for the ride as the land broke apart and moved.

Giant elephant bird = now **EXTINCT.**

OR

crossed to Madagascar from Africa **54 MILLION** years ago.

Lemurs still live on the island and **NOWHERE ELSE.**

Fossa

is **long** as a man is **tall.**

TOP PREDATOR on the island and it eats lemurs!

Other **NATIVE** animals on Madagascar

Mini-chameleon

can fit on a fingertip!

Now **4ᵗʰ largest** island in the world **248 miles** off the coast of Africa.

SKY ISLANDS

In some parts of the world, like Mozambique in Africa, there are forests on the tops of mountains. These are like islands in the sky, containing many unique animal treasures. It's very hard to get to them so the native animals have been able to stay hidden and safe—for now.

MINI-WORLDS

The different biomes of the world contain lots of ecosystems. An ecosystem is like a neighborhood of animals and plants who rely on each other to survive. A healthy ecosystem has loads of different animals and plants living in it. Ecologists use grids called quadrats to count and measure the creatures living in one small area of an ecosystem.

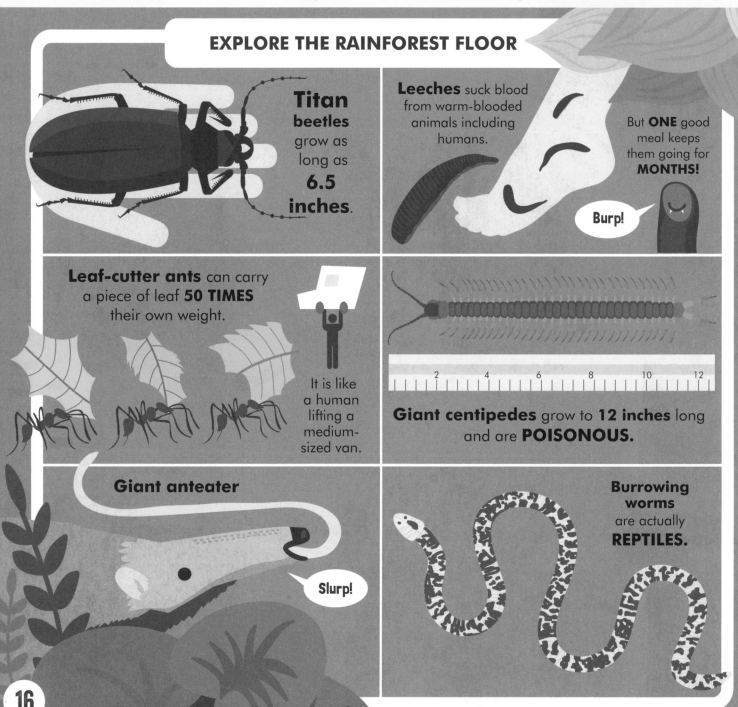

EXPLORE THE RAINFOREST FLOOR

Titan beetles grow as long as **6.5 inches**.

Leeches suck blood from warm-blooded animals including humans.

But **ONE** good meal keeps them going for **MONTHS!**

Burp!

Leaf-cutter ants can carry a piece of leaf **50 TIMES** their own weight.

It is like a human lifting a medium-sized van.

Giant centipedes grow to **12 inches** long and are **POISONOUS.**

Giant anteater

Slurp!

Burrowing worms are actually **REPTILES.**

WORKING WITH ANIMALS

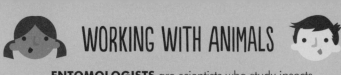

ENTOMOLOGISTS are scientists who study insects.
HERPETOLOGISTS study reptiles and amphibians, like snakes,
frogs, and turtles. Sometimes these scientists discover new species.

POND-DIPPING

AMPHIBIANS can live in **WATER** and also on **LAND.**

Frogs start life as eggs in the water.

Frogspawn (3,000 eggs)

Tadpoles

Froglets

Newts eat tadpoles.

Damselfly nymphs live underwater for **6 MONTHS** before **GROWING WINGS** and turning into flying adult insects!

Nymphs are young insects.

Pond skaters skip across the water surface **FAST.**

To match this a human would need to swim at **400 mph.**

Freshwater shrimps are **DECAPODS** which means they have **10 LEGS.**

WHO'S EATING WHOM?

Animals and plants all need food to stay alive. Plants and trees make their own food using energy from the Sun. Animals get energy by eating plants or other animals. These food pyramids show the way this energy is passed from plants to animals in three very different ecosystems. Lions are top predators on the savannah, but they would not survive if the grass did not grow!

Carnivore
mainly eats MEAT.

Herbivore
mainly eats GRASS.

Omnivore
eats EVERYTHING.

Insectivore
mainly eats
invertebrates (INSECTS).

Scavenger
eats the leftovers!

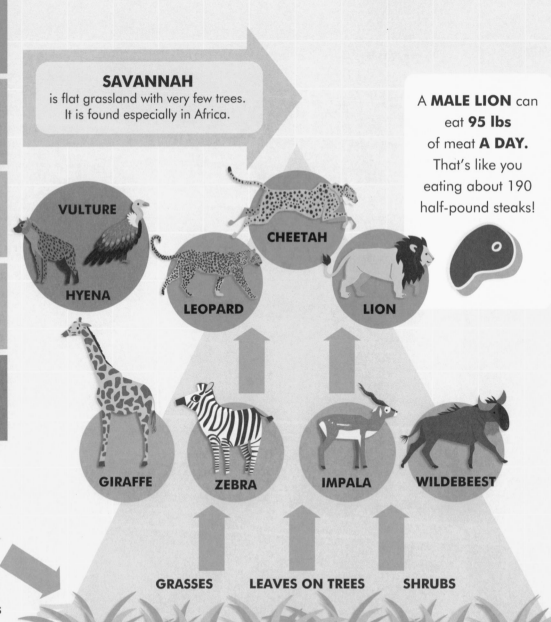

SAVANNAH
is flat grassland with very few trees.
It is found especially in Africa.

A **MALE LION** can eat **95 lbs** of meat **A DAY.** That's like you eating about 190 half-pound steaks!

VULTURE

HYENA

CHEETAH

LEOPARD

LION

GIRAFFE

ZEBRA

IMPALA

WILDEBEEST

GRASSES   LEAVES ON TREES   SHRUBS

SUNLIGHT
to make plants
and trees grow.

WORKING WITH ANIMALS

A **ZOOLOGIST** looks at animals in their own habitats as well as studying them in zoos or laboratories. They try to learn as much as possible about animal life on our planet.

POLAR BEAR

A **SNOWY OWL**
eats 3-5 lemmings
A DAY

=
**1,600
A YEAR.**

WOLF

SNOWY OWL

ARCTIC TUNDRA
is found north of the Arctic Circle. Only the top layer of soil ever defrosts in summer. Underneath is frozen **PERMAFROST**.

 **ARCTIC FOX**

 CARIBOU

 LEMMING

 **ARCTIC HARE**

GRASSES   **WILD BERRIES**   **MOSSES**

 **HAWK**

 **FOX**

OWL

TEMPERATE FOREST
is found in parts of the world where it is not too hot and not too cold.

Shrews can eat
ONE HALF TO 2 TIMES

their body weight in food **A DAY.**

BIRDS   **HEDGEHOG**   **SQUIRREL**    **SHREW**

PLANTS   LEAVES   FRUIT   NUTS   INSECTS   WORMS

19

HELPFUL ANIMALS

All animals were wild to start with, but humans have tamed (or domesticated) some of them.
For example, some animals are kept on farms so that they can provide us with meat, milk, or eggs.
The first animal that humans tamed thousands of years ago was the dog.

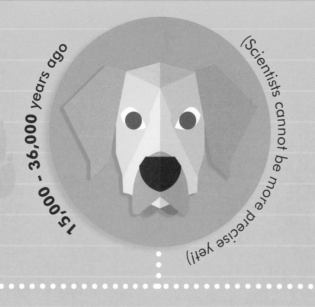

15,000 – 36,000 years ago

(Scientists cannot be more precise yet!)

12,000 years ago

People began
to farm.

36,000 years ago	30,000	25,000	20,000	15,000

People were building
shelters with branches,
bones, and skins.

DOGS ON DUTY

Sniffer dogs are trained to
find illegal drugs, guns, or
missing people.

Guide and hearing dogs
are trained to help blind
or deaf people get out
and about.

WORKING WITH ANIMALS

ANIMAL TRAINERS prepare animals for all sorts of jobs, from helping people with disabilities to detective work. The trainer must make sure that the animal understands exactly what to do when it hears or sees certain commands.

About 4,500 years ago

Stonehenge was built in England.

11,000 years ago

9,000-10,000 years ago

Humans started growing wheat and barley.

10,500 years ago

5,000 years ago

People invented writing.

10,000

5,000

Present day = NOW!

10,300 years ago

10,300 years ago

9,500 years ago

5,500 years ago

4,000 years ago

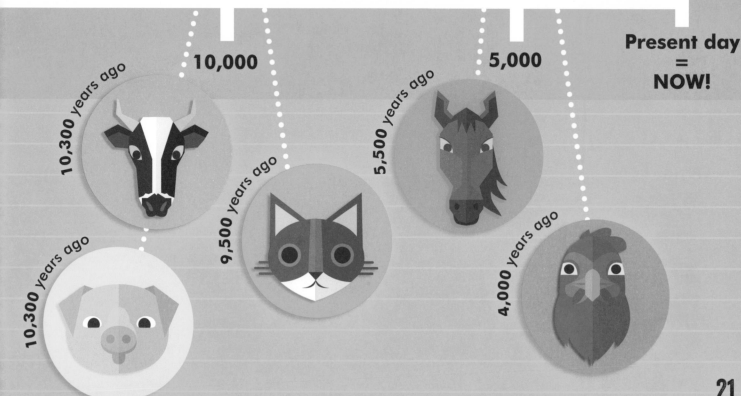

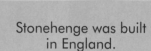

SAVE US!

Many animal species are in danger of dying out completely because humans are destroying so many of the places where they live. Some animals are also in danger because people hunt them for their horns, tusks, or meat. We need to take urgent action to save them.

OVER THE LAST 40 YEARS

The **TOTAL NUMBER** of **wild animals with backbones** (vertebrates) has gone down by

MORE THAN 50% = ONE HALF.

Freshwater vertebrates down by **81%.**

Land animals down by **38%.**

BUT in **protected areas**, like wildlife reserves, down by **18%.**

Sea and ocean animals down by **36%.**

PANGOLINS

8 species in the world.

Hunted for their scales and meat.

AFRICAN ELEPHANTS

The **LARGEST** animals walking the Earth.

Live in **37** countries in Africa.

SUMATRAN TIGERS

Found only on the Indonesian island of Sumatra.

WORKING WITH ANIMALS

CONSERVATIONISTS work to protect the natural habitats of animals. They often advise farmers on how to look after the wildlife on their land. **PARK RANGERS** work in parks and wildlife reserves. Sometimes they have to patrol a park to prevent illegal hunting. This is very dangerous work.

TAKE ACTION!

Look up information about animals in danger and how to help on the websites of conservation charities like the World Wide Fund for Nature.

Your class could adopt an endangered animal.

Help spread the message about how important it is to share our planet with animals and keep them safe.

Over the last **10 YEARS**

more than **1 MILLION** have been taken from the wild.

No one knows how many are left.

People hunt them for their ivory tusks. Their habitat is destroyed by mining and farming.

In the early **1900s**

there were **3-5 MILLION** elephants.

In 1980s

100,000

elephants were killed **EACH YEAR.**

Today there are only about **415,000** elephants left.

They are hunted and their forest home is being destroyed.

1978 **1,000** tigers

2018 fewer than **400** tigers

40 tigers are **KILLED EVERY YEAR.**

ANIMAL WORDS TO KNOW

ADAPTATION
A special characteristic that helps an animal to survive. For example, thick fur keeps animals warm in very cold places.

ANIMAL
A living thing that breathes. It can also move around to find food for itself. The Latin word *anima* means "breath" or "spirit."

BIOLUMINESCENT
describes a living creature that can make its own light. It does this to attract attention or frighten enemies. It also uses it to find prey in the dark.

BIOME
A large area of Planet Earth that has a certain climate and types of living things in it. Examples of biomes are grasslands, deserts, or forests.

CAMOUFLAGE
is the way that the shape or color of an animal can help it to hide from predators or disguise it while it is hunting.

CARNIVORE
An animal that only, or mainly, eats meat.

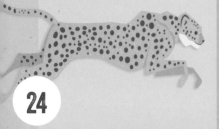

CLIMATE
The usual weather in an area of the world. It takes many years, even thousands of years, to change. It is not the same as weather, which can change from day to day.

CONSERVATION
means trying to protect wild animals and their habitats.

DOMESTICATE
means to tame an animal to keep it as a pet or on a farm.

ECOSYSTEM
This is like a neighborhood where everything has an important place of its own. It is made up of not only all the living things there, but also includes things like the weather, rocks, soil, or sand.

ENDANGERED
means animals that are in danger of dying out or becoming extinct.

ENDEMIC
describes animals that live in a particular area of the world, like the unique species in Madagascar.

ENVIRONMENT
The air, water, or land that people and animals live in or on.

EQUATOR
An imaginary line that runs around the middle of the Earth.

EVOLUTION
The theory that says all living things alive today developed (or evolved) from earlier versions that lived billions of years ago.

EXTINCT
An animal that has died out is extinct. It means that there is not a single one of them left alive anywhere in the world.

GESTATION
is the length of time that a mammal carries her babies inside her body before they are born.

HABITAT
is where animals live and make their homes. Animals can live in all kinds of habitats from boiling hot to freezing cold places.

HERBIVORE
An animal that mainly eats plants.

INCUBATION
is the length of time it takes for babies to be ready to hatch out of eggs.

INVERTEBRATE
A creature without a backbone or spine. Insects are invertebrates.

MAMMAL
An animal that breathes air, has a backbone, and produces milk to feed its babies. It also grows hair or fur at some point in its life.

MARINE
means to do with seas and oceans.

MIGRATION
The journey made every year by some animals. They travel to and from feeding and breeding habitats.

OMNIVORE
An animal that eats plants and meat.

OXYGEN (O₂)
A gas in the atmosphere that humans and many living things need to breathe.

PERMAFROST
A thick layer of soil that is always frozen. It is found in tundra areas of the world.

PREDATOR
An animal that hunts and kills other animals (prey) for food.

SPECIES
A group of animals or plants that are similar.

TEMPERATE
means not too hot and not too cold.

TUNDRA
The large, bare, and treeless area found between the ice of the far north and the forests of North America, Europe, and Asia.

VERTEBRATE
is an animal with a backbone or spine.